Also by Jane Routh

Books
Circumnavigation (Smiths/Doorstop 2002)
Teach Yourself Mapmaking (Smiths/Doorstop 2006)

Pamphlet
Places Like This (Gooseprint 2004)

Waiting for H5N1

Jane Routh

Templar Poetry

First Published 2007 by Templar Poetry
Templar Poetry is an imprint of Delamide & Bell

Templar Poetry
Fenelon House
Kingsbridge Terrace
58 Dale Road
Matlock
DE4 3NB

www.templarpoetry.co.uk

ISBN 9781906285067

Typeset by Pliny
Graphics by Palloma Violet
Printed and bound in India

For M., with my thanks

Acknowledgements

A version of 'Price' appeared in *The Allotment: New Lyric Poets* ed. Andy Brown (Stride 2006) and an earlier version of 'Forebear' was published by *The Rialto*.

Contents

Forbear

William Shackleton told the Justice the geese
were his. His wife agreed, and Isabel Ingham
could offer no proof: she had not liked
to clip patterns in wings, cut notches on webs.

Early next morning Isabel Ingham of Hurstwood
called up the rest of her flock and drove them lightly
along the bridleway, letting them graze
wherever she saw a patch of cleavers

and gathering as great an armful as she could carry
until they turned down the lane by William Shackleton's land
when she strewed it among her flock
causing such gabbling and squawking

that the geese in his top field, their feet
already tarred for Manchester, heard
the familiar voices and half-ran half-flew over the cop
in such a palaver of greeting

that though William Shackleton
called and called to the long line of creatures
walking back up the lane behind Isabel Ingham,
none heard his voice.

Rainmoon

Sometimes it's dark all day. It can rain so much
the fields are mud and you don't want to go out
but you have to, you have to carry buckets to feed trays.
You can't shake off the smell of wet wool,
your hands are numb, your head's down,
you're too cold to think but sometimes
even now, there's a day when the wind drops
and maybe that's warmth on the shoulder of your coat
and you drag the old bench into the sun, and stop.

The valley's clear for miles, the woods changing
winter greys for bud-colours, maroon and mauve,
and just when you're thinking *as good as it gets*
the midday quiet's pricked by a high thin wail
and there are five – no, up, higher – nine, yes nine
buzzards circling exactly above you and you tilt the seat
further and further until you fall and back-flip
into your aerial self, all of you hanging out
on a column of air crying *my valley my valley my valley.*

Egg

Candled against the light,
the egg is filled with the dark of a creature.
An airspace large enough to inflate lungs.

It was alive a four days ago.
Now it's silent: no tapping, singing,
not even cries of distress –

but to be sure, I float it
gently in cool water.
It makes no waves.

This was the last egg.
Leave it intact,
let it keep its death a secret.

All over the house, down-casings
from those who broke into life drift
and settle. This fine gold dust.

Hatch

Now we're worried about inbreeding.
I ring every number in the handbook
for new blood to run with ours.
Yes, it's a good year,
but the answer's the same:
Ring back at Michaelmas;
I like to see how they do.

A good hatch.
We need clean grass
and more shelters.
In the builders' merchant
the fork-lift driver shouts
What sort of polythene?
I say I'm housing goslings.

He switches off and climbs out.
I've been looking for some
for weeks. You selling?
As if words have a life of their own
I've said *Autumn, maybe;*
I like to see how they do, and he's
back in the cab: *You people.*

Price

Evenings, I drive the geese up near the house.
I sleep with the window wide, though it's cold.
It's only half-sleep, half my brain's listening,

listening for a change of tone, (they murmur
most of the night, on and off), listening for wingbeats,
for whatever danger sounds like.

Alarmed, I've run into the field three nights this week.
There's so much dew, it's like wading
through shallow water back to bed.

Down ripples in the grass, even in still air:
perhaps it's this makes you disbelieve a creature's
dead. Why do they take the heads?

John says you can call foxes up:
Shine a light in their eyes, and squeak. He demonstrates,
I practise, suck hard on the back of my hand.

He says I'll need to stay very still,
draw it in close for a gun like mine.
He says I should buy a rifle.

Corpse

Each evening as light drains from the sky,
we carry our offering down the orchard
and lay it head to wind to keep its shape.

Except it's headless. The body's undisturbed:
wings folded, feet tucked up, taken –
so we tell ourselves – in sleep.

We fetch it back before breakfast
and store it in the barn. Yes, soon,
soon it will smell too bad for us to handle –

but which of us will dare suggest we stop:
it's our insurance, this ritual
for a scavenging fox. Superstition

rules us: the first night it's missing
we'll lose another bird
and the whole season will pass

before we admit we were unsure
whether cries that woke us in the night
came from the orchard or our dreams.

Harbingers

A smatter of fieldfares and redwings across grey sky
so early they've returned to green woods,
fields lush with late growth. But no haws,
not a single berry on the tree outside my kitchen window.

o

The seagulls found dead in Finland
were shown to have died of starvation
though they carried, like most wild birds,
a low pathenogenic strain of AI.

o

Vigilance, biosecurity – words
in my own handwriting as naturally
as if I've used them for years.
I don't even know how to say *zoonose.*

Funeral

– cold air, a blackbird's ragged alarm call
then inside the porch, a chink
of brass handles on wood

Each little bird that sings
none of us need glance down for words
He made their tiny wings

a diamond pattern from leaded lights flits and fades
over plastered walls that lean toward the hillside
and skew the woodwork out of alignment

the building settling into its hollow between trees,
their leaves yellow, the bracken rust, rocks grey, all
still and wet, drip and slime and floods on the roads

the mist thinning as we leave, a sketch of estuary
far off below the fell, *as good a place as any*
no, don't be so English, it's beautiful, and she –

Migrations

Fieldfares and redwings have gone;
come early and moved on –

Ireland most like, he says, means
a hard winter to come.
o
Five Bewick's have returned
to the river downstream.

That's it. All done. No flocks
of dead besmirch our fields.
o
We've acquired one of those
great swirls of starlingsmoke.

Enthralled, I clip the bank
with my nearside wheel.
o
Irruption – I love the word. Signs are
from Scotland it will be a waxwing winter.

Last year they stripped the ornamental rowans
down at Riverside. And no one saw them.

FAQs

What is being done by whom?
Why are you arranging surveillance?
Does this mean that you are worried?
Should you really shoot down samples?
What should I do if I find dead birds?
If I leave my number, will someone ring me?
Am I at risk if I touch dead birds?
Can you guarantee birds I report will be collected?
Should I report dead birds hit by a car?
What if I can't get hold of anyone on Bank Holiday?
Where can I dispose of dead birds?
If you find 'flu in wild birds, will you kill them?
What are you going to do?
Who killed Cock Robin?
Do I have to worry?

UAQs

How do wild birds
spread a virus
across Russia
during the moult
when they can't fly?

How does a virus
cross Turkey
after Christmas
when wild birds
are wintering?

Why does a virus
pass from China to Vietnam,
along trade routes,
plaguing roads not
migration pathways?

Why does the virus
break out indoors,
among poultry
that never saw
daylight, or wild birds?

Nightmare

There was that Hitchcock film
The Birds. I could never bear
to watch it to the end.
Even now I see a gannet
diving for the kill as if I
were underwater, fish.
Birds
suddenly carriers of disease
that could mutate. And kill us:
birds,
            what we flee from.

Tetrad

On the top field above Birks below the moor:
      16 golden plovers,
      102 lapwings,
      127 common gulls,
      40 fieldfares,
      254 starlings

such exactitude not science, just the way numbers
add up in the hollows beyond stone walls
until the birds lift off and separate, the lapwings
flickering white-black-white in the sunlight,
starlings disappeared in their billow of blown smoke

all of them come from somewhere else,
all of them well: they like it here,
this winter, this view, the Three Peaks in cloud,
the human business of the valleys
mapped out below as far as you can see.

o

Three robins in every twenty minutes at a slow walk,
tit flocks in the woods nowhere to be seen today.
One buzzard, one kestrel; the heron in the meadow
by Furnessford Bridge where you'd expect.
More meadow pipits than I'd thought, but no goldfinches.
Wrens heard but not seen, counted anyway;
owls and the woodpecker silent.

Less steep than the new, the old road
winds steadily through the woods to the farm
under a sprawl of trees slayed by last winter's gale.
Apple trees at the top are too old to fruit;
rickety chicken huts, empty.
Farm dogs excited at the end of their chains.
Trussed tups. Heifers hoping for hay. Mud.

It's lunchtime and Sunday.
Harrison's feeding his sheep.
I'm counting the birds I tell him,
a man not given to conversation,
the folds in the map so worn
his fields fall into pieces
two kilometers wide.

Headlines

I panic. I'm gone all day,
come back with a carful:
thick rubber gloves that reach to the elbow,
tinned food in case we're zoned off,
toilet rolls to last three months.
I didn't know where to buy face masks,
forgot the British Standard number.

We no longer handle our birds,
the cool smoothness of feathers.
Clumsy in gloves and overtrousers
we feed them on concrete, swill down,
hose the yard and ourselves. *Don't* I yell at you,
when you rub your nose against a glove.
It's the closest we've come to falling out.

Stop. What's this about? AI HITS UK.
A dead parrot. In quarantine, down south.
We've been panicked. Our birds aren't
diseased. You say that's blazé: why shouldn't
they catch it? Think: there'd have to be a carrier;
we'd not be the only ones, and there'd be signs,
illnesses and − look how they feed.

Swan

A strange spring, late snow and the rivers in flood.
We're saying it's over for now, everything's back — if late:
curlews on the hill, tewits on the moor, the usual wagtail
running along the warm slate of the barn roof.
Only the swallows are not yet come. But that's all right:
Africa's too far, they're too frail to make it with disease.
And then there's the swan.

What on earth can we do? a friend rings
who hasn't thought about it until now:
How can you keep geese indoors?
I'm scared too, but my answer's full of websites,
zones and international industry,
though I know I'm no comfort: cull means
kill, and do you have to kill your own?

I'm looking through the window while we talk;
it's sunny, then it hails bouncy pea-sized pieces
I hear drumming on the ground before they get here.
The House Field's suddenly clear of geese —
off into the shelter of the trees.
When I put the phone down I stay there,
trying to get used to absence grazing the field.

Bliss

Heatwave. Water troughs shaded by trees:
rowan, birch – and wild cherries so weighted with fruit,
deer browse low branches.

I rinse out a trough and leave it to fill.
Run an arm under a bough, and you've handfuls.
The geese fly up, gulp red and black glints from the grass

shrieking for more, crowding into the moment
of what must be goose-paradise to them: the buckets full,
fruit from the tree, and a cherry-picker prepared to join in.

Frank heard the racket a mile up the valley,
rang later to check things were OK. *Merries,*
I told him, Grigson says was the old name for cherries.

Survey

This time we are to count plovers and lapwings
wintering inland on the moor, but for October
no boxes to tick or flocks to draw on the map:

the grass is too long. It's mild. Even the wind's
warm, though something sidereal's drawn
all the swallows away. This doesn't make headlines.

DEFRA's news is of butterflies on chalk grassland,
injurious weeds, and teenagers
making recordings of grebes.

What's changed? In the small print, the virus
is spread *by a variety of different pathways
including both legal and illegal trade.*

Riddance

One missing. A day like this — still,
with patches of sun, a few of the ash trees
yellow already — and I'm scrambling upstream
where the river borders Harrison's land.
I'm sweating. Midges are biting.
No feathers in the grass — just droppings,
two green-and-white piles on the beach.
The river's high. I edge between trunks
on the bank until mallard give me away.
She's not on the water. I need height,
struggle up an alder — at my age —
look, there, midfield: she's head down
cropping Harrison's grass. I drop
and suprise her: she's old and she's slow
and I can out-run her before she takes off:
I've got her neck, fold her wings and this time
I'll carry her home. What am I doing
on a day like this, green shit down my leg,
climbing a gate and telling a hissy goose
old beyond laying, how much I hate her
and how next time I'll leave her, glad to be rid.

Vaccine

She speaks good English.
Her flock is the same size as mine.
All her birds have had the vaccine.
They did not seem to feel the needle.
They are used to being handled.
She is happy that her birds will be strong.
What upsets her is the metal bands
strapped on their legs, thick and heavy,
stamped AI 2006 NL. This is the idea
of people who have not touched a goose.
She hears them, a new sound,
clink clink round the farmyard.
A stone was trapped, once a twig:
the birds were frightened.
She thinks about next year, more bands,
the other leg, her poor birds.
In 2008, they will have to cut
through metal. One person to hold
the bird and another to hold the leg,
a third to saw through bureaucracy.
I say I envy her: vaccination
in any language is better than a cull.

Exchange

I lean on a trunk. How does he
keep going? Frank puts down the axe,
takes out his pipe. He looks at me
as he lights up, that long performance,
then asks 'Any idea how many times
you've said *Aye* this morning?' 'I've not!'
'Aye, but things rub off both ways.'
'Don't tell me you're taking to poetry.'
'I mean those turkey sheds – what you said
more than a year since, it's right:
started indoors, not in the wild.'
'Aye, well…' 'That makes eleven.'

Coda

Dream

I should like to dream Mir Ali's dream
from six hundred years ago and in Tabriz
so, waking, I could show you how a flight of geese
becomes a script, how you can decipher
a bird's head in a flattened oval,
how a broad descending cursive gathers
strength like the downstroke of a wing
with an elbow at the point of rotation,
and how the thrust of a neck lengthens
to the boundary of balance, how the reed
dipped in its inks could stab beak-like
for those dots, the letters changing
like the shifts and combinations of a vee,
words given wings becoming poems
and still something wild about them
so that even the merest *heech* of a word   *[Persian: nothing]*
collects itself, angles back a wing shoulder
and stretches its neck to break from its cage.